the good
Date
guide

the good Date *guide*

Sarah Tomczak

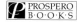
PROSPERO
B·O·O·K·S

Conceived and produced by
Elwin Street Limited
144 Liverpool Road
London, N1 1LA
www.elwinstreet.com

ISBN 1 55267 770 2

This is a revised edition of *How to be a Sex Goddess*
Copyright © 2003 Elwin Street Limited

Printed in Singapore

Picture credits
Photolibrary: page 22, 47, 56–7, 76, 93, 122,
125, 137
Corbis: 6, 28–9, 82–3, 140
All other images courtesy of Getty Images

Products supplied by Ann Summers.
Available from www.annsummers.com

There's something about her. . .

She's as hot as hell, and she knows it. She's the kind of girl who sashays down the street like she owns it, walking tall in her killer heels and classy threads. She loves her body, and she charms the socks off everyone she meets. Guys would do literally anything to get with her, she's a dating diva . . . and she could be you.

Sounds unlikely? You can drop that attitude for a start. All you need to do to fill your life with great dates, romance, and mind-blowing sex is to take the personal journey from girl to femme fatale—and this book is your guide.

No matter how un-diva-like you're feeling right this second, between these covers you'll find everything you need to turn yourself into a white-hot, femme fatale. You'll develop kick-ass confidence, learn to celebrate your shape, cultivate amazing style, and work it all to get everything and anyone you want. Of course being a femme fatale means having spine-tingling experiences in the sack too, and by the time you're done reading this, you'll have him begging for more.

How do I know all this? Easy. I am a queen of the dating scene. I'll admit it—men are suckers for my charisma and curves. I have the best friends ever and a job girls would kill for. My magnificent shoe collection would make you gasp with pleasure. It took a bit of work on my part (and a ton of cash for the shoes), but with the mind and body makeover found in these pages plus a pinch of determination and desire, I have reached the status of dating guru. Now it's your turn.

You're about to join an elite club of women, who not only have the world at their stiletto-clad feet, but who have the guts to take that first step too. . .

BECOMING A FEMME FATALE

The first secret of dating

1

Character is key

The first secret of dating is to turn yourself into a femme fatale, a powerful and attractive woman that men would give anything to be with. And the first thing you need to know about being a femme fatale is that there's no age restriction. True, with years comes a certain confidence—you become more at ease in your own skin and have lashings of life experience—but the sparkle and recklessness of youth are just as essential.

No matter what age you are when you pick up this book, you will find something in here that relates to you and, by reading it, you'll discover an even more insanely gorgeous version of yourself inside. In order to really qualify for the good date club, there are a handful of attributes that every girl must have.

Confidence

She has that self-assuredness that comes from knowing she's really something special. A femme fatale is never arrogant, but she has a cocky spirit that's derived from being happy with the way she looks and proud of the person she is.

Grace

It's hard to define, but grace is the calm, serene poise that a femme fatale is blessed with. It's an elegance—the ability to be discreet and dignified. The first and most important step toward gracefulness is to remind yourself to be good to people.

Strength

A femme fatale is brave and fearless. Even in the toughest of situations, she has the courage to remain true to herself and fight for her cause. She does not apologize for her beliefs, she does not quit and she does not let anyone, or anything, get her down.

Humor

A femme fatale can laugh at herself . . . and she has a beautiful laugh, whether light and twinkly or loud and uproarious. Humor gives her good perspective, strengthens her spirit, and makes her amazingly good company. Her joy is infectious and she gets a kick out of cracking everyone else up too.

Charm

There's nothing as enticing as a femme fatale who's got her game on. With her flirtatious, alluring, mesmerizing ways, she can have anyone wrapped around her little finger—but that's such a nice place to be. When a femme fatale gives you attention you feel like the sun is shining on you; nothing beats the tingling warmth of her charm.

"We are all of us stars and we all deserve to twinkle."

MARILYN MONROE

Loyalty

Once you've found a femme fatale (or she's found you) you have a friend for life. She'll defend you in an argument, never forget your birthday, let you rant and rave hysterically at her, and throw you the most fabulous parties. She'll never forget you and never let you feel unloved. Best of all—she'll turn you into a femme fatale too.

Intelligence

Degrees and doctorates aren't necessary, but a femme fatale is nevertheless well-read, sharp, and knowledgeable. She can hold a good conversation, she's a great listener, and she's open-minded. She's interested and soaks up information, from popular culture to hard-core politics, and she can wax lyrical on almost any subject. If there's something she doesn't know, she's happy to admit it and determined to find out more.

It's an incredible woman that possesses all the qualities mentioned above. But the truth is, you really are something special. Even if you feel lacking in one area, time, experience, and tenacity are all you need to help polish and hone each attribute to your satisfaction. Above all, a femme fatale has a wild, vivid, irresistible spirit and that's what makes her stand out in a crowd.

Get the look

Blonde, brunette, redhead? Lithe and leggy or a ton of curves? None of that matters. Dating success doesn't depend on a specific body type or hair color. Girls that just ooze glamour come in all shapes and sizes. Nevertheless, there are some key features that all dating-savvy girls do possess: firstly, they all know they're a femme fatale.

Their hair, while being groomed, is never over-styled. Forget the hair-sprayed helmet look—her mane is more unruly (she made bedhead sexy). And her eyes have those thick sooty lashes (the kind that defy mascara) that she's perfected looking through in a sultry manner. She's totally comfortable in her own skin and she's not above flashing a little of it now and then. (She does this so casually, it's almost like she didn't mean it to happen . . . almost.) And her body is toned and strong—not hard-core buff, not stick-insect thin, but it definitely doesn't resemble Jell-O either.

Every dating guru possesses amazing style. It's as simple as that. The clothes she chooses always manage to flatter her figure and she pulls off outfits in ways that mere mortals could never hope to achieve. Her hip-ness permeates her closet and she can suddenly make anything cool again—from vintage tweed blazers to skinny Bermuda shorts. Whether she splashes out on designer cashmere or raids her great aunt's chiffon scarves, a femme fatale will instantly appear the height of chic. She's equally capable of pairing leather with spiked heels and looking downright dirty, too. Famous femmes fatales, and the kind that you see on the street, all have the ability to start a trend; there's a blend of confidence and panache that helps them lead the way.

Most femmes fatales develop a signature style of their own. Their clothes say a lot about the women inside. Don't be surprised if the attire's a little racy; femmes fatales usually are. But demure kitten heels and a pencil skirt can give a glimpse of just as much va-va-voom.

She doesn't just attract men, she attracts everyone. Talk to a femme fatale, and you'll instantly adore her. It will be her combination of charm and street smarts, her wicked sense of humor and irresistible bluntness. Plus she'll be flirting with you (femmes fatales love to flirt). Her sex appeal is electric and she can use it to her advantage. You'll notice she's self-assured and spirited; she knows what and who she wants and there's no doubt she has the ways and means to get it.

You may feel a tinge of envy—how on earth can she be so confident? Does she ever feel low? It's good to know that femme fatales are excellent actresses. Even when they're not feeling on top form, they'll still have a glossy veneer. They'll never wallow in sadness or disappointment—they're always looking for that silver lining.

Women with that special *je ne sais quoi* can be found everywhere. They're in countries where women have the freedom to be powerful and equal to men. They have no inhibitions and are fearless in following their dreams. The women who are lucky in love often have amazing jobs, or are pursuing their goals and achieve great things. You can find these incredible women in every walk of life—from actresses to teachers, athletes to traders.

And as soon as you start to think like them, you'll realise that it's not just about attracting the opposite sex, it's about pleasing youself and believing in yourself. This is the first step to good dating, because this is the first step to self confidence.

Having it all

Dating is not a part-time job. It's not just about sizzling in the bedroom, or deciding to pluck your eyebrows more regularly. It's also about becoming empowered, and heating up every aspect of your life. What are your wildest dreams? What do you wish you could achieve at work, in your relationships, or with your body? Once your head's in the right place, everything else will follow and will fit perfectly like a magnificent, life-size jigsaw puzzle.

On the inside: you will feel more confident and ready to face new challenges. You'll be more open-minded about trying new things, like making a career change, taking a belly-dancing class or turning up at a party solo. You'll be more content with the way you look, you'll lose your hang-ups and will learn to love (instead of despise) the bits that make you different.

On the outside: you'll become a style maven! You'll wear clothes that make the most of your body in colors that look like they were made for you. You'll have fantastic hair, silky-soft skin, and you'll apply make-up like a pro. Your personality will shine through your fashion choices and women will be begging you for tips on how to look as good as you do.

In relationships: you'll be in control. You'll have the feminine wiles to snare any man you want and you'll always leave him entranced. Your romances will be long, lusty, and full of life. With your friends, you'll be loyal, loving, and generous—but you'll never be walked over.

In the bedroom: you'll always be satisfied. You can forget the sexual hang-ups—you'll know exactly what you want, how to ask for it, and how to enjoy it. You'll be just as in-tune with his body and will use that to stroke, touch, and tweak every bit of him until he can't take any more. And if things don't go according to plan? You will have the class and confidence to handle that situation too.

In your career: the sky's the limit. You'll decide what you want and you'll have the drive to go out and get it. Your boss will look at you differently, you'll command respect in the workplace, and promotions and pay rises will be yours for the taking!

INSIDE...OUT

Bring your strengths to the surface

2

It's all in the mind

No matter what you may be thinking right now, these powers of attraction are inside you and this chapter is all about letting them out. Confidence is key, but feeling self-assured and learning to love yourself isn't always easy. The tips and suggestions over the next few pages will help change the way you feel. Performing a mind overhaul is the toughest part in the journey but once you've achieved this, everything else will fall effortlessly into place.

Look at any successful woman and you'll see she oozes confidence. She's happy to be in her skin and she has the spirit and sureness to take on new challenges, standing up to anything that's in her way. Don't be fooled into thinking that she was naturally blessed with these gifts—although it may be harder for some people to achieve than others, confidence is everyone's for the taking.

Got to have that cup of coffee before you step into the shower? Read magazines from back to front? Have a secret love for show tunes? These are the things that make you irresistibly unique, but you have to discover them yourself before someone else will love you for them. We constantly grow and develop as people, but are often too busy living life to sit back and acknowledge the changes. Take time out for yourself—traveling alone is the perfect way to find out what you're really about. Can't take six months for a self-discovery trip to Goa? Book a week at a yoga retreat or a beach resort and go solo. Haven't got the time or money? Take an entire day to yourself every few weeks. Decide how you want to fill the time, find out what makes you happy, and discover what makes you, you.

Once you realize the kind of person you are and what interests you, expand on the things you like and develop them further. You'll be far more self-assured when talking about your love for paintings, for example, if you spend time reading art magazines or visiting galleries. Plus, there's nothing more appealing than a woman who pursues her passions—from skating to knitting. It's also a great idea to subscribe to a daily or Sunday newspaper. Keeping abreast of current affairs not only widens your horizons, but gives you better control over your own thoughts, and means you won't feel intimidated in social situations.

Use this new-found awareness of yourself and the world around you in other areas of your life. Learn how to read situations with friends or colleagues, judge your place in the group (or office) dynamic, and follow your convictions. Understand when you are truly comfortable in a situation and what makes you feel good and try to replicate this as often as you can. Try to develop a positive mental attitude—look for the good in people, the silver linings behind the dark clouds, the highlights of an otherwise bad day. Don't care too much what others think of you and don't judge yourself based on anyone else's opinion. Like yourself for who you are and don't change for anyone.

TRY THIS NOW!

Remember to give yourself time and space. Find ten minutes each day to sit quietly and alone and allow yourself to feel peaceful and happy. Close your eyes and picture yourself on a beach or in the countryside, until you feel totally relaxed and at ease with yourself.

Right here, right now

Often our self-worth is determined by ifs. "If I was 5 lbs lighter I would like my body," or, "if I got a promotion I would be doing well at work." It's great to have goals, but basing your self-belief on something that may not happen is never going to make you feel like an amazing person. Instead, concentrate on the stuff going on in your life right this second that you're pleased with: "I went to the gym today," or, "I had a productive meeting with my boss."

Whenever your goals feel hard to obtain, stick to the right here, right now and focus on feeling good about what you're doing to reach them. When we need a little support we tend to turn to those closest to us. So while on the hunt for your inner femme fatale, let your friends or your parents become your own pep squad. They already adore your generous nature or salty sense of humor. By reminding you of this, they'll reaffirm that you're special. Surround yourself with positive, sparkly people and let their optimism rub off on you.

When you're looking for a little guidance, find a role model. She's the woman who can work a room, pass off a store-bought gateau as her own, and ask her boss for a pay rise. She's got loads of confidence and watching her is like getting the whole scoop on what it's all about. Don't feel weird about asking her for advice—femmes fatales are always willing to share their knowledge. Ideally she'll be a few years older than you too, so she'll be able to give you some pointers from her own experience.

Treat yourself

Vogue editor and legendary fashionista Diana Vreeland wore red. Jackie O chose oversize shades. Audrey Hepburn opted for shift dresses and ballet pumps. So how do you make the most of what you've got? Every woman should have a signature style—it's like a flash of personality, a small fanfare that lets people know you've arrived.

Your signature can be anything—maybe you have fantastic legs (in which case a miniskirt is the only way to go), you could adore magenta (so always have an accessory in this hue), or perhaps you have a fascination with chandelier earrings (collect them and wear every pair).

Decide what looks good on you, what you enjoy wearing, and embrace it. Give every outfit a twist, make it personal, own your clothes. Your signature doesn't have to be expensive, either. Say you covet vintage bags; scour flea markets to find the right pieces to match your outfits. They're usually cheaper than anything you'd find in a department store and you can be sure no one else will have them.

Everybody loves to be spoiled, but don't sit around waiting for that bouquet of long-stemmed flowers or the bottle of Champagne to land on your doorstep, take the matter into your own hands and show yourself some affection. Make your love gifts regular (once a week should do) and big or small depending on your budget.

Sometimes splurging out on an expensive coffee is all it takes. Other times a weekend away could be in order. You'll soon discover what constitutes a pick-me-up and you'll know when you deserve that extra something special. Reward yourself even if you're not feeling blue—pampering shouldn't just be reserved for down days— boost your self-worth and celebrate just being you.

Budget

The new paperback by your favorite author.

A bottle of nail polish in an eye-popping hue.

Coffee and a flaky pastry from a fancy French patisserie.

An apple martini in a swanky bar straight after work.

A bunch of mauve tulips.

A taxi home from anywhere.

Blowout

A pair of designer shoes that weren't on sale.

A St. Tropez tan at an upscale beauty salon.

Dinner at the poshest restaurant in town.

A weekend in a faraway city.

Vintage jewelry.

A bottle of Champagne with no good reason to drink it.

Faking it

Take the fast track—make everyone believe you're already the sassiest, sexiest femme fatale before you've even got there. Sure, inside you may feel like a quivering bag of nerves, but nobody else has to know that. Do your best red-carpet-at-the-Oscars impression—act like you totally belong. You can fake it a number of ways:

🌀 *Act naturally:* But be subtle about it—try too hard to be someone you're not and you'll blow your cover. Follow other people's lead from the smallest things like what to drink, to what to talk about or wear. The best way to appear to fit in is to become one of the pack. Once you've developed the nerve, then you can let your wildness shine through.

🌀 *Oscar-winning performance:* Alternatively, show off your acting skills and play the most confident, gorgeous, feisty version of yourself (remember the way you feel in your sexiest outfit after a heady glass of champagne) and replicate. Pretend you're this luscious lady and no one will know you're a fraud. They'll respond to your faux aplomb and will figure you were just born bold.

🌀 *Walk the walk:* Dress to dazzle and, instead of sloping into a room, strut. Look people in the eye when you talk to them, then laugh at their jokes, and flirt outrageously. Be calm, stand tall, accept a compliment gracefully—do all the things you know a femme fatale would do. Remember, practice makes perfect, so try this routine a few times and soon it will feel like second nature. After a while you won't even be faking fearlessness . . . you'll be the real deal.

FEELING HOT, LOOKING HOTTER

How to see a femme fatale when you look in the mirror

3

Shape up

Who's totally happy with her body? Seriously? How many celebrity interviews have you read where a seemingly stunning, crazily thin woman is complaining about how she doesn't always feel beautiful or that there are parts of her body that need improving? It's insane. Time and again this proves that, no matter how tall, short, thin, or fat a girl may be, she can be unhappy with herself. Surely it would be better to love your figure and celebrate its size and shape—whatever it may be.

Flick through any fashion magazine and you're bound to get a little depressed by the constant images of jutting hipbones, perky breasts, and mile-long legs. But who really looks like that and why does your own body image have to mirror it? The first step to embracing your own figure is to stop comparing it to the airbrushed images you see in magazines or on TV.

Work it

Let's face it—none of us is perfect when it comes to body shape. Most of us have curves that are never going to go away (and why should we want them to?), but that doesn't mean we can't make them more toned and luscious. Apart from making you stronger, fitter, and healthier, exercise is a great way to improve your body image.

For a start, when you exercise, your body releases endorphins into your blood stream, which enhance that feel-good factor. Secondly, when you start paying attention to how fit or strong you are, you stop thinking about how your body looks and focus instead on what your body can do.

We should get physical every day. That doesn't mean hard-core aerobics sessions or even pumping iron at the gym 24/7, but it does mean being active and raising your heart rate for at least 30 minutes a day. Walking or hiking outside is great, as are cycling, swimming, even your half hour grinding on a dance floor. Becoming a gym bunny is a good way to motivate yourself, especially if you work it into your daily routine by always attending certain classes. Keep yourself on the straight and narrow by getting a friend to sign up too—it's a lot harder to make excuses and take off early for a glass of wine when she's already practicing her yoga stretches.

TRY THIS NOW!

In surveys women frequently rate their face as the most attractive part of their body. Psychologists argue that this is because women are used to seeing their face and have come to accept the way it looks. Try standing naked in front of a mirror three or four times a week and focusing on what is good about your body. You will soon come to love the uniqueness of your physique in the same way you love and accept the individual details of your face.

Bite me

Dieting. It's tedious, depressing, and rarely works—95 percent of dieters regain the weight they lose in one to five years. There's nothing fun about restraining yourself from food you really want to eat. But then, knowing you've just polished off an entire pint of ice cream is not much fun either. Eating any food in moderation is okay.

Most women base their self-worth on how good their body looks and how "well" they've eaten that day. But defining food as good or evil is like hitching the bus to Bluesville. Instead of deciding how certain foods make you feel emotionally, focus on how they make you feel physically. Does a bacon cheeseburger make you feel nauseous? Do you feel bloated after a huge plate of pasta? Do you crave chocolate just 20 minutes after you've eaten mashed potatoes? Notice how eating starches (white bread, pasta, potatoes, and rice) late in the evening makes you feel heavy and uncomfortable, making it even harder to sleep, while leafy green vegetables, like spinach, or proteins, like chicken or fish, leave you full without feeling gross and overstuffed. Make your dietary choices based on what tastes good but also on foods that leave you refueled and energized.

If you do want to get slimmer, make sure you do it sensibly. Fad and food exclusion diets are definitely not the way to go. From the Atkins diet to the raw-foods diet, to the blood-type diet, to the cabbage-soup diet, the truth is, no matter how much weight you lose digesting these bizarre food combinations, you'll put it all back on again once you go back to your regular eating habits.

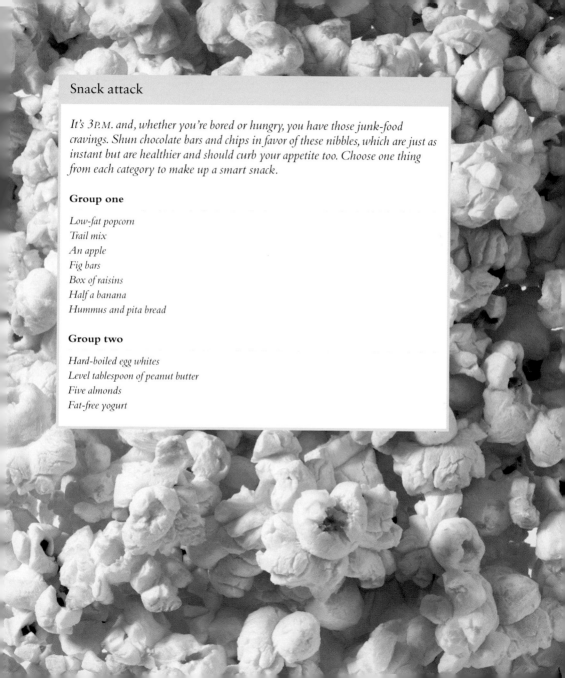

Snack attack

It's 3P.M. and, whether you're bored or hungry, you have those junk-food cravings. Shun chocolate bars and chips in favor of these nibbles, which are just as instant but are healthier and should curb your appetite too. Choose one thing from each category to make up a smart snack.

Group one

Low-fat popcorn
Trail mix
An apple
Fig bars
Box of raisins
Half a banana
Hummus and pita bread

Group two

Hard-boiled egg whites
Level tablespoon of peanut butter
Five almonds
Fat-free yogurt

The only way to lose fat is to burn off more calories than you consume. So, to lose pounds the healthy way, combine exercise and good eating habits. The best way to drop weight is to have four small meals and two snacks throughout the day. This will keep your metabolism at a constant and stop you from feeling hungry. In every meal balance complex carbohydrates like fibrous vegetables and whole grains with lean protein like fish, turkey, and chicken. Each portion of food (protein or carbs) should not be bigger than the surface area of the palm of your hand (one of the biggest mistakes we make is with portion control).

Steer clear of starches, junk food, and alcohol. Don't aim to, or expect to, lose more than 2 lbs a week, or the chances are very high that you'll regain this weight. See healthy eating as a way of life— once you have reached your desired weight, stick to the same healthy foods you've been consuming but allow yourself a treat once in a while. Remember, you'll pile the pounds back on if you resort to a daily menu of burger and fries. Dieting should not make you miserable, so if you're having real problems with yo-yo eating plans see a nutritionist for even more solid advice.

The other thing to keep in mind is, if you combine diet and exercise, you may not notice a big weight loss on the scales as muscle (which you should be building by exercising) weighs more than fat. Throw out your scales and judge your progress on how your clothes fit instead.

Be good to yourself

Fulfilment in life is all about balance. You may be the first person to order Champagne, the last person to leave the dance floor, and the only one to suggest doing it all over again the following week. But you also need to know when to cancel your plans so you can snuggle up under a cashmere blanket and rent black-and-white movies all weekend if you need to. Even if you're bursting out of a birthday cake in a lamé bikini one minute (figuratively speaking), you need to acknowlege when to take things down a notch and give yourself a chance to recharge.

The den of Zen: who hasn't gone a little overboard on the booze, cigarettes, and drugs at some point in her life (or the last few weeks)? Such nights are hazy memories at best, while the mornings are hell on earth. Chances are, during every hangover you vow never to drink again, and yet the promise is broken the moment a martini is placed in front of you. No matter how cool blowing smoke rings may look, cigarette breath, nicotine-tinted teeth, and smoke-scented hair are disgusting. And alcohol may be a great icebreaker, but getting so trashed you're out of control is foul. To avoid becoming drunk and undesirable, drink a glass of water between every alcoholic beverage (fool friends into thinking it's a vodka and tonic) and try to limit yourself to one cigarette an hour (instead of one every five minutes).

Get some shut-eye: call it beauty sleep, growing time, or a good rest. Whatever it is, your body needs it. Eight hours' sleep a night is a great way to look and feel gorgeous in the morning. Don't get enough and your skin, digestive system, mental alertness, physical energy, and entire well-being will be messed up. So find your eye mask and retire to your boudoir this instant.

Sun sinners: while there's no denying a tan makes you look like a slimmer, healthier, more gorgeous version of yourself, the risk of developing skin cancer means it's so much safer to fake than bake. Get the femme fatale look with a sunless tanning cream instead (if you can't handle D.I.Y., visit one of the spray-on tanning booths which are popping up in salons everywhere). If you have to step out into the sun, only do so once you've covered yourself with at least a shot-glass worth of S.P.F. 15 or higher and reapply every two hours. Floppy hats and huge shades are so Italian Riviera and make great sunshades too.

Stress-fest: every high-flying, fast-paced woman is going to get a little stressed-out; it can't be helped. When you're juggling a job, a relationship, a social life, a fitness regime, future goals, and everything else that goes along with being young, hip, and on your way up, you're bound to freak out at times. Reduce the tension, anxiety, and insomnia by learning how to plan your time better, by creating space for yourself (this is where the cashmere blanket and old-movie renting come in), and by accepting that every ball can be dropped a few times. Life does go on.

Keep it real: the girl who will only drink water, eat raw carrot sticks, make gym dates, be in bed by 10P.M. and slathers on S.P.F. 45 every time she leaves the house is no fun to hang out with. She's not a femme fatale. The girl who indulges in the odd frozen margarita, can beat you in a running race, and is proud of her round, swingy breasts is as sexy as hell.

Perfectly polished

Notice how you always feel good after a visit to the hair salon? You can be wearing your most unbecoming top and your baggiest sweatpants, but if your hair looks great, your skin glows and you feel like a million dollars. It's the same with a manicure. A French polish or a slick of red can turn a plain old T-shirt and jeans into a classy ensemble. The crazy thing is, most women see a trip to the salon to get someone else to blow-dry their hair or paint their nails as a frivolous luxury.

A dating diva, on the other hand, knows this is essential grooming. What's the point in splashing out on a pair of strappy heels, only to accessorize them with hard skin and battered toenails? And why spend an hour perfecting your eye shadow, only to top it off with fuzzy, unruly brows? Start putting aside maintenance money and scheduling weekly salon visits. If this still seems extravagant, justify it with any of the following reasons.

You'll look good: shiny hair, polished nails, shaped brows, and stubble-free legs are the added extras that make you that bit glossier and better groomed. They'll also come in handy when you bump into your ex-boyfriend in the grocery store, or an old college acquaintance at the movies. Don't save looking your best just for that big party or a wedding, make it an everyday occurrence.

You'll feel good: you already know that when you feel confident inside you glow on the outside, so look at grooming as your secret ammo. Catch a glimpse of your recently highlighted hair in the mirror and it could be the thing that stops you crawling miserably back into bed in the morning, refusing to face the world.

You'll enjoy doing it: reclining in a comfy chair while somebody else pampers, primps, and preens you—what's not to love?

Budget

Buy an at-home French manicure kit. It contains two shades of polish and stickers to place on your nails to help get those perfect white tips.

Blowout

Go to a salon for your French manicure. Get a pedicure while you're at it (amazing with open-toe sandals). Tip: make your polish last longer by applying a clear top coat every other day.

Touch-me hair: there's no one look that every style queen should have, but there is one thing they all have in common—the kind of hair you can't resist running your fingers through. Desirable tresses are glossy, healthy, and a tiny bit unruly (au revoir straight-laced chignons). The other important thing to remember is to have a distinct style. Whether it's platinum blonde with a blunt fringe, a side-swept part with face-framing layers, or a messy, pixie crop—your cut should be bold, not blah. Find one of the best hairstylists in your city and pay him or her a visit. It may feel like a lot of money, but remember this is something you wear every day. Do it . . . because you're worth it.

Kiss and make up: smoky, come-to-bed eyes, or glossy lick-me lips? The choice is yours, but you can only have one, because playing up both features is overkill and just not hot. By day, keep it simple with a dab of concealer and a dusting of bronzer, but when night falls, shake things up a little. Decide whether you'll draw attention to eyes or lips. If it's eyes, smudge a charcoal shade over your lids, or take style cues from the 1960s and apply a pastel color wash with a sweep of black liquid eyeliner. Take a walk on the wild side with fake eyelashes (the individual lashes are harder to apply but the end result is worth the effort). For lips, make them matte or glossy and choose any shade from poppy to peony. Never, ever line your lips with a dark pencil and fill with a lighter shade (so not sexy) and, while on the subject, leave the glitter, stick-on jewels, and temporary tattoos to the kids too.

Body language

Now we've established that your body is actually gorgeous, it's time to discover the best way to show it off. This means highlighting those extra special bits and diverting attention away from those less-than-perfect areas. The best way to do this is by using the tricks of a fashionista's trade—cut and color. Highlighted below are some of the simple rules to follow, depending on your body shape, and it's definitely worth taking yourself out for a mammoth shopping trip to try on everything and anything which will help you determine which styles work best for you. Once you've found the cuts and shapes that most flatter your figure you can base your entire wardrobe around them. If you want to avoid fashion faux pas before you've even made them, remember that learning what doesn't suit you is just as important, and this applies to fabrics as well as the cut of a garment.

Color is key—no matter how classy beige may be, if it washes out your skin, it will never look elegant. For a femme fatale, skin is always in, but try and avoid the obvious—legs and cleavage will turn heads, but show something unexpected and temperatures will really soar. Try highlighting the curve of your back, your collarbone, or exposing your neck instead.

Once you know exactly what suits you, you can start experimenting with each season's trends by adapting items to fit your look and only buying clothes in cuts that suit you. If the shapes are simply wrong for you, keep your clothes classic and incorporate hip accessories into your look instead (this is a much cheaper way of staying fashion forward too).

Hourglass

- Scoop-neck tops accentuate your decolletage. Avoid high necks—they look better with a small bust.

- Flat-fronted pants keep you streamlined and a boot cut balances your figure.

- Low-rise pants that sit on your hips are also a perfect fit for you.

- Rather than hiding your shape under layers of chunky fabric, stick to light flowing fabrics like silk that will skim over your body instead of hiding it, or wear clothes with more structure.

- Dazzle with accessories on your skinniest body parts, like bangles on your wrists, dangling chandeliers on your earlobes, and jeweled thongs on your feet.

- Choose longer-lined jackets and Burberry-style macs and pair these with slim-fit, tailored dresses, or light camisoles and dark denim jeans.

Petite

↻ Add virtual inches to your height by dressing in one color and wearing high heels, but don't overdo the height. Slingbacks are a good option.

↻ You look great in patterns and frills so choose tops with adornment. Because you have a small frame be careful not to break up the line of your clothes with belts or short skirts.

↻ A fluid silhouette is very flattering (a simple, one-color dress would achieve this).

Pear Shaped

↻ Wear darker colors on the bottom half of your body to slim it down and draw attention upward.

↻ Patterns, frills, corsages, and adornments look fantastic—but on your top half only.

↻ A wide, boat-neck top will balance your curvy hips and bottom.

↻ Avoid full, circle skirts that make hips look bigger, stick to a pencil skirt or long boot-leg pants.

Tall and Leggy

🌀 Create the illusion of curves by choosing pieces that belt or tie around your waist.

🌀 Break up long legs with capri pants or pencil skirts and heels with ankle straps.

🌀 Horizontal stripes are adorable and you can pull them off with aplomb.

🌀 If you're proud of your pins, there's nothing sexier than a mini, but keep your shoes flat to avoid looking trashy.

Large Tummy

🌀 Wear light gauzy shirts or dresses with an empire line, which fit under your bust then skim over your stomach.

🌀 Direct the focus onto your fabulous legs by wearing a baggier shirt (to cover your waist) over a miniskirt (to show off the pins).

🌀 Invest in underwear with a stomach-control panel to flatten your figure—perfect worn under a dress and so much simpler than breathing in!

🌀 Don't tuck in your shirt or wear anything belted or cropped at the waist—move your accessories higher up and wear a wide-necked top with cool earrings, a chunky necklace, or a chiffon scarf.

More dash than cash?

Dressing like you've just stepped off a catwalk doesn't have to cost a supermodel's salary. Be savvy and stylish by knowing that there are ways to get the look you want without having to survive on ramen noodles for the rest of the month.

Take a long, hard look at your closet and gather together everything you haven't worn in the last two years. Organize a stoop or garage sale; keep your prices low and people will flock.

Log onto an Internet auction site. These are great places to sell unwanted designer items (the more covetable the piece, the higher price it will fetch). Alternatively, if there's something you've been obsessing over, these could be the places to find it—at a much cheaper rate. Beware when bidding though—don't bother placing your bid until 10 minutes before an auction ends (or you'll probably get outbid and will just push up the price) and make sure that you don't get caught up in a bidding frenzy, so spending more than you wanted to.

Consignment, goodwill, and thrift stores are great places to hunt for stylish items with rock-bottom price tags. Get friendly with the owners and they'll put aside things that you might want. The neighborhood in which the shop is situated often reflects the quality of clothes you'll find inside, so check out goodwill stores in up-market areas for designer clothes that have barely been worn. If you don't like the idea of buying second-hand clothes, stick to accessories like bags, scarves, and costume jewelry.

10 essential items

Oversize sunglasses

Slipping on a pair of shades is like adding instant glamour to any outfit. Avoid wearing indoors or on a rainy day—there is such a thing as trying too hard.

Butt-defying jeans

Every girl has a gazillion pairs in her closet, but you should only wear to death the ones that make your thighs look slimmer and your butt smaller.

Amazing coat

Think of all the cash you spend on great clothes, only to cover them with the same old black winter coat. Invest in a hip overcoat in a unique color—a pink dogtooth check, a camel herringbone, or a simple cream wool. Pay attention to interesting details like a belt, leather piping, or oversize pockets. You can keep the clothes underneath simple and let your overcoat show off your supreme sense of style.

Slinky dress

Choose something in silk or jersey that clings to your curves. It doesn't have to be black, but you'll get more mileage out of a dark color, so try chocolate or charcoal gray instead. This should be the kind of dress that you can slip on for an impromptu dinner with killer heels, or wear after a day at the beach with leather flip-flops and tousled hair.

Lingerie

No matter how good you look on the outside, if you're wearing a ten-year-old washed-out bra your mom gave you, you'll never feel sexy. Invest in some breath-taking underwear and you'll relish not only the knowledge of your hidden finery but also the sumptuous feeling of lace and silk against your skin.

Figure-flattering bikini

Easier said than done. Be prepared to try on a ton of different styles because the one that you expect to be least flattering could actually be the opposite. When you've found a swimsuit that you really do feel good in, buy more than one—there are far more enjoyable things to do on the beach than worry about how your butt/belly/boobs are looking.

Diamonds

They're every girl's best friend but they don't have to cost the earth. Check out antique fairs for good prices on small diamond trinkets and, if your budget really doesn't stretch that far, buy a small pair of Cubic Zirconia earrings and, if anyone asks, lie (the smaller they are, the more convincing this will be!).

Cashmere sweater

Classic, comfortable, and timeless. Wear it with a suit to work, with a leather skirt for an evening out, and with your jeans when you're chilling. Start off with a simple style and color, like a black crew or roll neck, and then build your collection.

Expensive watch

You wear it every day, so make an investment and see how it increases the value of your entire outfit. Buy something simple that complements the rest of your wardrobe and you'll be glad you did— a classic silver Gucci watch will add va va voom to your look every day of the week.

Killer heels

Strappy sandals with skinny heels jazz up a pair of jeans and turn a pencil skirt or slip dress into a dynamite ensemble. Tip: Make sure you can walk in them; there's nothing wrong with heels so towering that they'll only take you as far as the first taxi, but you must also have a pair that can be worn on the dance floor.

Something simply amazing

Every now and again you will see something gorgeous that
you can't live without. It will take your breath away. It will evoke
visions of you sitting on a yacht in Monte Carlo wearing it, or
attending a New York Gala with it tied around your neck (or
feet if you're salivating through the window at Manolo Blahnik).
When you see this wonderful thing, you shouldn't hold back, but live
out your fashion fantasies instead, even if it's only once a year.

These beautiful, expensive things are the items you'll care for
and covet for years to come. These are the things that you'll pass on
to your grandchildren. When you buy, don't give in to the guilt
(unless your credit card is maxed, in which case you should
probably ignore this bit), but enjoy every second of the pandering
sales assistant, the crisp logoed tissue paper, the glazed shopping bag.
For almost all femmes fatales (except the mega-rich) these moments
are few and far between, which is why they should be savored and
most definitely indulged.

If you've read this entire chapter and decided none of it is relevant
to you because you simply don't have the occasion or environment to
care too much about style—think again! There are no excuses for
living your life in tapered jeans and faded sweatshirts, or for wearing
your hair scraped back in a ponytail every day. Don't just dress for
yourself or your friends, dress for the girl that glances over
admiringly on the train every morning, and the guy in the deli, and
all the other random people who pass you in the street and think
to themselves, "Wow, she looks amazing." Dress to impress
everyone—always.

KISSING FROGS

The highs and lows of dating

4

Date expectations

Dating is fun, fun, and even more fun isn't it? After all, while your coupled-up friends are spending their evenings together in front of the television, you're out dining at the best restaurants and catching the latest shows with countless gorgeous guys.

Your life is so exciting that everyone else is looking to you to regale them with your stories of spine-tingling kisses and electrifying encounters. What about the passionate police officer who succumbed to your charms after pulling you over for speeding, the handsome men who slip you their business cards on your way to work, and the cute postman who nervously asked if you were free for a drink sometime?

While it all sounds fabulous, in reality, dating is more a rollercoaster of highs and lows, with countless stomach-churning loop the loops along the way.

A heart-stopping clinch can't prevent rejection. That passionate police officer may just decide, inexplicably, not to phone you after all (which is his loss by the way). Even having countless men at your beck and call can ultimately prove tiresome.

And just as rapidly as you found yourself luring men like a bright light lures moths, you may stumble into a dating drought in which it feels like all the eligible men have taken an extended holiday to Mars.

Every girl needs to know the rules of dating, from the bar right through to the bedroom. And you need to know what you want too. Are you looking for a fun fling with a guy? Or are you looking for someone who might become a boyfriend? Maybe you're not sure— that's OK too. Dating can be complicated.

Cue the first date

You've found a man who interests you and, after a volley of witty banter, he suggests going out for a drink. He's hotter than hell, so of course you agree. First dates are much easier if you have something to focus on, other than attempting to fill three hours with non-stop witty conflab.

🌀 Do give a guy a chance.

🌀 Don't write him off because you hate his shoes!

🌀 Do go somewhere relaxed, ideally a venue that creates conversation.

🌀 Don't do dinner on the first date.

🌀 Do talk a little about yourself, such as your family, job, and aspirations.

🌀 Don't start revealing your relationship history and philosophies on life.

🌀 Do ask him about his life.

🌀 Don't interrogate him about his ten-year life plan.

🌀 Do have a good time.

It's a guy thing

Before you can have a date, first you must find a man. So what should he be like? He has to be charming, confident, witty, and intelligent. He has to be wildly attractive (to you anyway), and whenever you're near him you should feel an insatiable urge to rip his clothes off and have wild sex with him right then and there. Yet, despite his erotic allure, he should also be a gentleman—nobody has a problem with being bought flowers, taken out for dinner, or even having a door held open for her once in a while.

He should also appreciate your own wit and wiliness and see you as an equal. Above all he should adore you, not in a patronizing puppy-dog way, but in the way that he knows you're always the most gorgeous woman in the room and he's lucky to be with you.

And whenever he's with you he's laughing at your jokes, marveling at your knowledge, and fantasizing about peeling off your underwear, all at once.

Okay, all this might seem a lot to ask for—charm, brains, and killer good looks all in one package? That is a rare treat. Looking for the perfect guy means having relationships with a few flawed ones along the way—and that's part of the fun of it. The truth is, no one is going to be everything you want at every moment of your life. Keeping high expectations is a good thing, but throwing in a pinch of reality is even better.

The key thing to remember when dating is finding a guy that you dig. When a man approaches you in a bar, chats you up, and then asks you on a date, it can be very flattering and hard to turn down. But the next thing you know, you're stuck having dinner with someone you have nothing in common with—and certainly don't expect to be getting frisky with—just because he asked you.

Rule number one is remember number one—it's all about you.

Desperately seeking a sex god . . .

So where do you find this rare hunk? Surely he can't be the guy sitting next to you on your morning commute, or the man flicking through the bestsellers beside you in the bookstore? Maybe he is. Finding the right guy should be fun, not a depressing, deplorable pursuit. It's a good idea to accept now that you may kiss a few frogs before finding that prince, but if a "frog" happens to be a gorgeous European tourist who needs someone to show him the sights (and in exchange will help you perfect the art of French kissing), maybe you should suffer a little for romance!

Keep your eyes open and follow the fizzle. If you catch a guy's eye and feel a sexual friction, or you find him so attractive that you have to concentrate on listening to him, instead of just imagining him naked, or he just makes you laugh and laugh—it's worth pursuing a date. There's nothing wrong with going after what you want— men love strong, driven women and, by making the first move yourself, you'll avoid the syndrome where you date guys you're not even into just because they asked you out.

When you're eyeing up potential partners, there are lots of places to check out. Bars and clubs are an obvious choice, but the loud music means your opinion will be based mostly on their appearance and dancing skills. Nevertheless, thanks to a few cocktails, this is often when you're at your least inhibited so your slay-him outfit and ragga-style grinding could really pay off! You want to hang out with a guy with similar interests to you, so start looking in the places you frequent most—the gym, a tennis club, your favorite pool hall, the theater that shows art-house films. Equally, set-ups through friends are always worth pursuing. They're like a more trustworthy matchmaking service (without the yearly membership fee).

And there's always the Internet, just make sure you don't put yourself in any danger and always arrange to meet in a public place first.

It's raining men

A surplus of men is a bit like going to the supermarket and being confronted with dozens of different brands of chocolate biscuit. Is it possible to tell which one is the tastiest from looking at the packet? We all know how disappointing it is when something just doesn't taste quite as delicious as it looks.

Too many men too little time sounds like every girl's dream, but if you're in this position, you need to learn to pluck out the good ones from the crowd.

Sorting through the riffraff

If only rotten men showed the same obvious signs as a piece of rotten fruit. Unfortunately, no matter how discerning you are, or how finely tuned your radar is, there is no definitive way to sort through men. And remember, even the most badly behaved men can turn over a new leaf once they meet their perfect match.

However, follow these four basic rules and you can avoid wasting your time with men you really don't deserve.

"I'm bored of dating men who turn out to be wrong for me. Emotionally, it's exhausting. I need to stop saying yes to every man who asks me out and learn how to be more selective."

JENNY, 25

Rule Number One—Only date men you're attracted to

Don't let feeling flattered lead you to accept a date with someone you don't really fancy, or you'll end up dodging his after-dinner kisses and wishing you'd spent the evening with your friends instead.

If you don't think he's gorgeous, or he doesn't make you laugh and you don't feel that frisson of excitement as he speaks, then just politely decline his offer. Remember, you've got more than enough men on your hands without those you don't even fancy.

Rule Number Two —Only date men who are single

If he's married or got a girlfriend, forget it. You don't need a few compliments from a two-timer to boost your confidence. If he says he wants to leave her to be with you then fine, that's his decision. But he needs to act on his words before you date him. Dating a man recently heartbroken can have its problems too, so make sure he's made a clean break.

Rule Number Three—Only date men who treat you well.

Listen to your common sense. If he never rings when he says he will, flirts with anything in a skirt or ignores you when he's with his friends then forget it. There is even less reason to spend time wondering if you can change him (by the way, the answer to this is probably not) when you've got more men on the go than you can handle anyway, no matter how handsome he is. Send him on his way.

Rule Number Four—Don't date men who are . . .

Grumpy, moody, aggressive, sarcastic, egotistical, arrogant, big headed, materialistic, monosyllabic, and pompous.

Surviving a date drought

Men are like buses—one minute three come at once but once they've vanished over the horizon, you're in for a long wait for the next.

If you're just sitting at home waiting for Mr Right to ring, then turn back and start this book all over again, implementing all the advice on how to boost your confidence and unleash your inner femme fatale.

If, however, you've followed all our tips, become irresistible and mastered the X-factor, then you've hit what is known as a dating drought. While you're waiting for the rains to come again be good to yourself. No man's land may be barren of the opposite sex, but it doesn't have to be devoid of fun. It's easy to become lack lustre during a dating drought, so it's up to you to keep your spirits high.

Just because there's no man to shower you with compliments doesn't mean other people aren't doing exactly that—you're probably just not noticing. Listen to what others say, and take a mental note of their compliments. You can reassure yourself too—think of things that you are proud of and don't succumb to worries about "never getting a date again."

For now at least, what you do is all about you, which is something anyone in a relationship will tell you to relish while it lasts. Put yourself first, give yourself treats. Now you're not spending money on dates and new outfits for dates, you can splash out on a weekend at a spa with the girls or that pair of Jimmy Choos you're lusting after.

And don't forget, the more you're out and about, and the more fun you have, the more likely you are to come across new men who will be unable to resist you.

Sometimes when you're not looking for or expecting "it," "it" lands on your doorstep.

"Since moving to a new area, I've been single for 18 months. I can't believe I thought a new neighbourhood would mean more chance to meet men—I've got to the stage where I don't think I am EVER going to meet someone EVER again. Even worse, my confidence has taken a dip, especially when I see all the good men on the arms of beautiful women. I'm beginning to wonder if I'll be a spinster for the rest of my life."

CARINA, 22

"My total lack of dates is driving me crazy. No man seems even remotely interested in me, and I'm spending all my evenings at home with my cat. This isn't how dating was meant to be. I thought I'd be going to bed with gorgeous men, but instead it's just me and my mug of hot chocolate."

LOLA, 36

SECRETS OF SEDUCTION

How to make him melt

5

Feel hot, hot, hot

Before you head out for a night of sex (or light flirtation) in the city, you need to remember your femme fatale status. Hopefully, by now you should be feeling pretty good about yourself. Over the past few chapters you've developed confidence and self-assuredness, you've accepted your body (and hopefully even decided it's damn sexy), and you know how to look your best. Think of all this as your honey—men will buzz around you simply because you're giving off happy, sassy, sexy vibes.

Prepare for an evening out by putting on your favorite outfit—the one that you know makes you look amazing. Spend a little extra time getting ready—don't rush—it's important that you're feeling as hot as hell on the inside, so you can project it.

When you get to the bar, or club, think about the way you stand or sit, notice how you interact with everyone else. The worst thing you can do is sit in the corner of the bar with your head drooped, trying not to catch anyone's eye, and looking miserable, or feeling awkward. The best thing you can do is sit tall, or, even better, stand (it's easier to feel empowered and confident). Smile a lot, look friendly and approachable. Catch people's attention, exchange a joke with the barman when you buy drinks, enjoy feeling people's eyes on you. Bask in the admiring glances, relax and savor the attention. Chat with your friends, but keep an eye on the males surrounding you. They will approach—there's no doubt. And when they do, it's time to really work the magic . . . which brings us to flirting.

How to flirt—a crash course

Flirting should be like breathing—second nature. Once learnt, it's a technique that you can use time and again to get what you want from any situation. Master flirting to perfection, and you will be able to ensnare any guy you like, for as long as you want him.

The most wonderful thing about flirting is that the whole process of making an amazing guy feel good about himself by flattering, enchanting, and simply letting him know that you find him attractive, will inevitably get you feeling downright gorgeous yourself. All guys respond to flirting by reciprocating, which makes for a mutual love fest. So while you're working to make him feel special, he's reacting by switching on his own charm.

Before you know it you're both feeling like a million dollars, which simply adds to the sexual attraction and is bound to end with one of you asking for a date. Sounds blissful doesn't it? And it is so easy to master flirting. It's just a simple combination of three essential ingredients—body language, sassy chat, and confidence—all executed with a dollop of good humor. Once you've got these basic aspects skillfully covered, the world is your oyster.

TRY THIS NOW!

Book yourself onto a speed dating night with a friend. This is a perfect opportunity to perfect your flirting technique. Don't worry if it isn't going too well, you only have a limited time slot with each guy, so you can alter your approach with the next one.

Body language masterclass

Body language is the most powerful language of all. According to experts, non-verbal language communicates over half of what we really mean, while tone of voice contributes 38 percent. Words themselves can convey as little as 10 percent of the message we're trying to get across.

The good news is it's pretty easy to recognize the basic signals we all give out, and learning to read these clues will help you avoid wasting time on second dates with men who aren't really interested.

Posture

If he's sitting up straight and looking relaxed, then he's feeling comfortable and having a good time. Even better, if he's leaning towards you —this means he's beginning to build intimacy with you. Slouching or yawning are big warning signs, even if he claims to be tired. Tired or not, the type of man you want to be with will be able to summon up his energy for a special evening with you.

Eyes

Holding eye contact is another positive sign, especially if his pupils are dilated and he is blinking more frequently, both signs he is attracted to you. Also look out for "the eyebrow flash." When we first meet someone we're attracted to, we raise and lower our eyebrows very quickly. If they fancy you, they'll flash their eyebrows back. Incredibly, this subtle gesture is found in cultures across the world. If his eyes are wandering, especially toward other women, be worried—it's an indication that his thoughts are not with you.

Lips

Touching his lips or licking his lips subconsciously is another sign he is interested. People usually touch their face and chin casually to draw attention to their lips because kissing is the first stage of intimacy.

Conversation

While you chat, his tone should mirror yours, showing your words and feelings are being heard. He should also mirror your speed and tone when he answers you, picking up the pace as the conversation becomes more animated and lowering his voice appropriately when it becomes more serious. Nodding can be a positive thing, but too much nodding coupled with a blank stare means you're talking to a brick wall. He's probably thinking about something else.

Arms and hands

We're frequently told that crossed arms is a defensive posture, but this isn't always the case particularly if it's cold! A more accurate indicator is the hands, which tend to be facing upward and open when people are relaxed, and are clenched and face downward when they're tense. We also tend to point our hands toward the person we're interested in.

Legs and toes

Just like with the arms, crossed legs don't always mean a lack of interest—sometimes it's just more comfortable to sit that way. However, are his legs generally pointing in your direction? If he finds you attractive, they will be whether they're crossed or not. Toes too, are a good indicator. When someone is feeling excited or energetic, their toes tend to move, or make little circles.

Here are some tame (and some downright saucy) techniques that will help seal the deal.

⟳ Pay his appearance a compliment—avoid the cheesy (and obvious) "do you work out?" and draw attention to his great shoes, slick haircut, or cool watch instead.

⟳ Hold his gaze for a few seconds longer than necessary.

⟳ Touch him "emphatically" when you talk to him (the thigh or waist are hot spots and show that you're doing more than just making your point).

⟳ Find an excuse to flash some skin. Innocently show him the scar you received, aged 13, during hockey practice—which just happens to be on your thigh/shoulder/hip.

⟳ Whisper in his ear—this is easy to do if you're in a noisy bar, harder if you're somewhere quiet. Tell him a secret and you're doubling the intimacy.

⟳ Talk about something sensual, like how you prefer to sleep naked or that a massage turns you on.

⟳ In a busy environment, invade his personal space slightly—the closer you stand, the more obvious your motive. When you're just millimeters away he'll have no doubt of your intentions.

Making the moves

Forget waiting for a guy to notice you. If you've seen someone you want, go out and get him. Here, are a few dating success stories to show you how it's done.

"When the guy I liked told me he wanted to bleach his hair I offered my services. I'd never colored anyone's hair before, but that was irrelevant. I made him take his shirt off (so it wouldn't get bleached) and that combined with wet, soapy skin and intimate contact meant it wasn't long before we were making out."

SUSAN, 24

"In a bar recently, I bought a guy a drink, dropped it off with him and said, 'Hi. I don't want to interrupt your evening, but here's your next drink on me, and if you'd like to join us, we're sitting over there.' He came right over."

DENA, 28

"I recruited my current boyfriend for my street hockey team. Being the captain gave me the chance to pluck him from an opposing team and convince him to join us instead. I was already on a power trip then, so it was easy to take the next step and ask him out."

REBECCA, 25

"I got talking to a guy at a bar one summer and invited him to my annual barbeque fiesta the following weekend. I had no plans to throw a party, but after he said yes, I had to. I spent a fortune and hosted this major soirée. Luckily he did show up, and he never discovered the party was thrown for him and him alone."

SOPHIE, 31

Sizzling dates

Not ready for the sex bit yet? Bowl him over with your classy
seduction skills by suggesting one of these dates—dinner
and a movie has never looked so average.

Brunch

Choose a classy, old-school hotel. It's more affordable and less
contrived than a dinner date, plus there's nothing sexier than
getting tipsy on mimosas before midday. Who knows when
you'll need to book a room?

Boating on a lake

Lie back and let him do the work. Falling in the water isn't
essential, but if the weather's warm, it's the perfect excuse to
drop anchor and "sunbathe" while your clothes dry off.

Salsa night

Don your heels and a ruffled skirt. Split a jug of sangria. Feel the
heat of his body pressed against yours while you step forward,
back, and cha-cha-cha.

A picnic in the country

Pack a hamper and take a drive, find a grassy meadow, lay out a
blanket, and treat your man to strawberries and Champagne—
and perhaps a frolic in the fields.

Sledging

Embrace your inner child and go whizzing down a powder-covered hill together on a sledge. Finish with a snowball fight (don't let him win), an icy make-out session, and hot toddies by the fire to warm up.

Roof-top cocktails

Slip into a black minidress and shimmy up to the top of your roof. Enjoy a glittering night time view of your city while you drink martinis together.

Everyone gets nervous . . .

Don't let your nerves paralyze you. Here are some simple tips to help your date run smoothly. If it's not going to plan, you can always take a moment in the bathroom to "powder your nose" and reassess.

- If you can't face the thought of awkward silences over a dinner table try a date that will spark conversation – a museum exhibition, a hike, a festival, carnival, concert, or film.

- Maintain eye contact and remember to smile.

- Give your date your full attention, ask questions, and be a good listener.

- Don't be distracted by cell phone calls or messages, or other people.

- Think positive and be friendly. He's probably nervous too, so make allowances for this when judging his behavior.

- Make sure you talk about yourself, but don't tell him all your problems, hog the conversation, moan, bitch, or complain too much.

- Even if the date is not going well stay friendly and calm, you can always make a polite excuse—remember to be kind.

- Don't promise further dates or phone calls if you don't mean it.

⟡ Don't give into pressure (sexual or other) or let yourself be pushed outside your comfort zone if you're unsure or if it doesn't feel right.

⟡ Don't obsess over how the date is going—relax and enjoy it.

His place or yours

You've had an amazing night together, have shared a few bottles of wine, one or two naughty secrets, and a few lusty gazes. What's next? There's nothing wrong with inviting him back for a night cap—but it's good to set the boundaries right from the start. Given half the chance, men will usually be through the door and on your sofa quicker than a tom cat in spring. How long they stay is your choice.

If you definitely don't plan on having sex with this guy, let him know right away that this really is just going to be a Cointreau and coffee affair. Putting the parameters out there early on means you won't feel pressured later. If you do crave some casual sex, that's fine too, but be savvy about it—never go back to a guy's apartment if you've only just met him. Instead go back to your place. If you have a roommate, let them know, or if you're leaving your friends at a bar, get one of them to call you in 30 minutes time. It may ruin those first throes of foreplay, but so much better to be safe than sorry.

If first-night sex is unappealing (because there are still some ladies among us), keep him hanging on with the promise of what's to come. Give it all up on the first date and you have nothing left to tease him with. Play a little hard to get and you'll pique his desire, and leave him desperate to see you again.

IN THE BEDROOM

Taking things further

6

Too sexy?

So you've survived the date, and you want to take things further.
It's time to discover your femme fatale self in the bedroom.

The first thing to remember is that there's no such thing as too
sexy. Being a femme fatale means being in touch with your
emotions—all of them—right down to your deepest, darkest,
dirtiest desires. Confidence in bed is just as important as in the
other aspects of your life—but it's sometimes harder to gain
because it is such a sensitive area. You're stripped bare (literally
and figuratively) and your emotions (and breasts) are totally
revealed. This is a vulnerable position to be in and it takes a pretty
sassy lady to feel at ease and take control.

It's no surprise that women reach their sexual peak in their mid-
thirties—it takes that long to feel okay about your body and to
sleep with enough guys to a) know what you're doing and b) know
what you want him to be doing. But, as a femme fatale, you don't
have to wait until you hit the big three-0 before becoming a minx
in the sack. With experimentation and assertiveness you could get
everything you want (including that mind-blowing orgasm)
right now.

One of the most important things to remember is that men love women's bodies. When you're thinking small boobs, he's thinking pert breasts; when you're panicking about saddlebag hips, he's greedily running his eyes over your curves; when you're trying to avoid highlighting the cellulite on your butt, he's trying to caress your perfectly-formed posterior. By the time you're naked, a man's eyes are glazed over with lust. Just remember that he's viewing you in soft focus and let your worries blur away.

Sex is not about how your body looks from a certain angle, it's about what turns you on and makes you feel good, what sends sensations through your body and how hot you can get, when the lights go out (or stay on, either way). No matter what anyone else says, loving sex and wanting lots of it is totally healthy; you should enjoy that orgasm—you deserve it. So stop thinking about it and get on with doing it.

"God gave women intuition and femininity.
Used properly, the combination easily jumbles the brain
of any man I've ever met."

FARAH FAWCETT

Create a sex den

It might just take one night before you indulge in a mad sex marathon, or maybe you've been holding out for a few dates, making him crave you even more. Whatever the situation, sooner or later you'll probably be letting a man into your boudoir. But who can get horny when surrounded by dirty washing, smelly sneakers, and harsh overhead lighting?

Prepare your lair for a night of passion by setting the right atmosphere. Start by clearing away the clutter, then focus on creating coziness. Ignore the ceiling light in favor of more flattering lamps and candles (not too many though, or it may look like a séance). Choose a warm color for your sheets—burgundy or chocolate brown are good picks—and add a scattering of small cushions (useful for propping up hips, heads, and other body parts). Music is a great mood enhancer so a stereo with a remote control and an assortment of slinky CDs are a good investment. A gorgeous

Budget

Part with a little cash for a basic full-length mirror from a DIY home store. Place it at the end of the bed in prime position to view your sexual antics.

Blowout

Splurge on an ornate mirror, the size of your bed and have it fixed to the ceiling overhead. It's daring, decadent, and deliciously dirty.

cut-glass decanter filled with water for quenching that mid-sex thirst is the perfect final flourish.

Once you've brought a guy back to your place, you can turn your seduction up a notch. Now it's not about cutesy ways to let him know you're interested, but more about teasing, tantalizing, and turning him on so he'll do just about anything for a piece of you. Being romantic and coy is great on a date, but this is your chance to get down and dirty and show him the real woman inside. See the next chapter for the lowdown on taking things further still—from perfecting your own sex skills to receiving that to-die-for orgasm (no vibrator necessary).

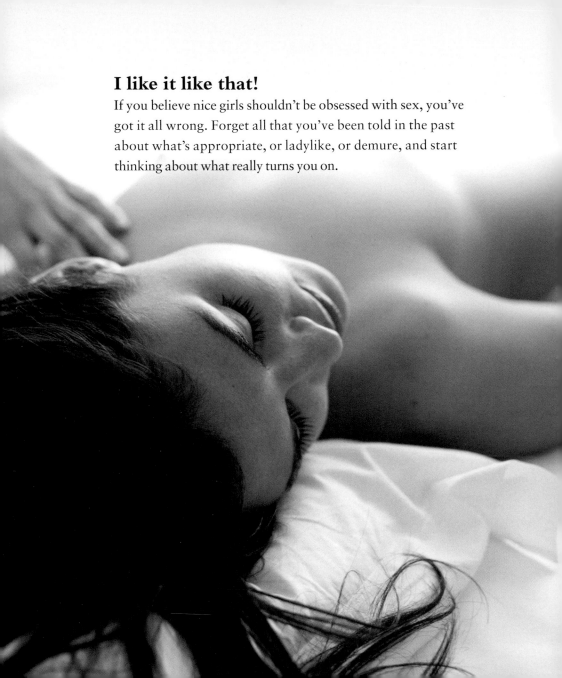

I like it like that!

If you believe nice girls shouldn't be obsessed with sex, you've got it all wrong. Forget all that you've been told in the past about what's appropriate, or ladylike, or demure, and start thinking about what really turns you on.

The simple fact is, if you don't know what makes you orgasm, how can you tell anyone else? Here are some things to try to help you get aroused.

Masturbating is a sure-fire way of finding out exactly what turns you on and how you most enjoy being touched. It's also great for relieving stress, making you feel good (an orgasm releases endorphins), exercising your vaginal muscles, and increasing the number of orgasms you'll actually have *avec un homme*. Here are three ways to masturbate for maximum effect:

The clitoris

Rub your clitoris lightly in a circular motion or back and forth. The tip of the clitoris is ultra-sensitive so if this is too intense, rub your pelvis up against a pillow or your mattress, or spray jets of water from the shower between your legs.

The G-spot

Slide two fingers inside you and reach up toward your stomach. You'll find your G-spot 1–2 inches up, a spongy patch of skin about the size of a quarter. Gently but consistently rub it in a circular motion.

The A-spot

This is just above your G-spot but below your cervix. It's a smooth, extremely sensitive area about the size of a nickel that will really respond to gentle rubbing.

Big girl toys

Forget Barbies and stuffed animals, there are just a handful of aids you should have close to your bedside.

Vibrators

Whether it is something small and slick that can fit in your clutch bag or a massive machine with numerous heads and oscillating speeds—you're bound to find a vibrator to suit you. Hold it against your clitoris or labia for sizzling sensations.

Porn

Re-enact a blue movie together, pop a tape into your video recorder and keep up move-for-move. Playing it in mute means you can ignore the cheesy dialog and concentrate on the action instead.

Toys

Love eggs wiggle around orgasmically when you insert them inside you. Ribbed condoms give you that extra friction during sex. Lubricants make all body parts slippery and easy to insert, and clit ticklers are pretty self-explanatory. All can be found at your local sex shops—a slew of trendy sex shops have made these toys stylish, so there's no need to enter the stores incognito.

Positions

The *Kama Sutra* might be a good jumping-off point, but your own imagination should take you a whole lot further. The more flexible and gymnastic you are, the more amazing positions you'll be able to achieve and if it feels good, who cares what it looks like?

Fantasies

Spill your secrets and get him to do the same, not only will you learn a few tidbits to turn him on, you'll also improve your sexual communication and probably strengthen your relationship in the process.

TRY THIS NOW!

Head out and get yourself a "butterfly." This is a small vibrating disc that you slip over your hips and under your panties. Once in place you can stay in your bedroom if you like, but why not leave it on while you go about your daily chores. This way you can orgasm while shopping for groceries, with the sex scenes at the movies, or when things get really dull at work.

Don't ask, don't get

Now that you know what makes you quiver between the sheets (and that lesson seemed nothing like studying), you have to get that information out in the open. It can feel awkward telling a guy that his seduction skills aren't quite doing the trick but, knowing what hot, toe-curling pleasures await you, how can you lie back, smile sweetly, and let him tinker with your intimates with the tenderness of a car mechanic? The important thing is not to make his confidence (or anything else, for that matter) droop with a bitchy comment.

Instead of telling him what he's doing wrong, focus on how he can get things right. Be upfront—ask if he wants to find out exactly what drives you wild, and when he says "yes" (because he definitely will), use his hands and your own to squeeze and stroke you in all the right ways.

Once he's seen how easy it is to make you melt, he'll definitely use the same tricks again. If this feels way too forward, you could always try keeping quiet during the less erotic moments and making the appropriate moans and groans when he gets it right. This method may take longer, but after a while he's bound to take the hint. One last option: spill your turn-ons over email or during a late night phone call. You won't have to deal with the awkward face-to-face thing, but you'll get your feelings across with some sexual frisson thrown in too.

How to please your man

Nothing feels better than knowing you are driving a man insane between the sheets. Being a sex vixen and being able to bring him effortlessly to the brink of orgasm is pretty damn empowering. Ask him what tips him over the edge—it's great foreplay (little gets him more aroused)—and you're bound to get turned on too simply by knowing how much carnal pleasure you're giving him.

If you want to throw a little of your own creativity into the mix, here are a few surefire things he'll love in the sack (even if he doesn't quite know it yet).

⟳ *Having his ears licked:* This is definitely one for the early stages of foreplay, but remember that a man's ears are so much more erogenous than a woman's. It will drive him wild and leave him begging for the real action.

⟳ *Having his nipples tweaked:* Chances are you don't give his chest as much attention as he gives yours (but be gentle, he's just as sensitive as you), so gently rub his nipple in between your thumb and forefinger, or nibble at it, or swirl an ice cube over it.

⟳ *You sex:* Tell him exactly where and how you want him. He may not want to have you bark orders at him every time you get dirty, but once in a while he'll get off on being overpowered by you and playing the sex slave.

🔥 *You masturbating in front of him:* Guys love the voyeuristic aspect of watching a woman touch herself and it's the perfect way to show him how to swirl your fingers around your clitoris and rise to an orgasm.

🔥 *Shoes:* No doubt you've seduced your man by parading around in a push-up bra and black lace thong, but have you ever considered ditching the threads in favor of strappy stilettos and a whole lot of skin? It works every time.

🔥 *You on top:* You've probably tried this facing him, but twist around so you're facing his feet. Men are also obsessed with a fine butt, so he'll really get off on staring at yours.

🔥 *Noise:* You don't have to compete with Kim Catrall's howling in Porky's, but a few enthusiastic moans and groans will only intensify his own excitement—especially if you really mean it.

🔥 *Make it public:* It's wild and dangerous, but what man hasn't fantasized about a woman slipping discreetly under the table, unzipping his fly, and giving him head in the middle of a fancy restaurant? It's essential that he keeps his cool so as not to give the game away.

🔥 *Suck some ice before giving him a blow job:* This works even better if he doesn't know you're doing it—he'll experience an icy rush instead of the warmth of your mouth he was expecting.

🌀 *A little pleasurable pain:* Whips and handcuffs aren't everybody's cup of tea, but he's guaranteed to enjoy you grazing your nails lightly up his inner thighs.

🌀 *Give him a full-body massage—using your entire body:* He'll be driven wild by the warm scented massage oil and feeling your breasts, feet, and shoulders rubbing against every part of him.

🌀 *A Brazilian wax:* It may be a little painful but all that smooth skin on display never hurt the girl from Ipanema...He'll go crazy for the uninterrupted view of your vagina he'll be even more eager to get down there and feel the softness against his cheeks.

SEXPERTISE

Something extra for sex perfection

7

Playing the big league

Once you've mastered the basics of sex, you can get onto the serious stuff. On the following pages, you'll find the kind of moves that set a femme fatale apart from the average girl. These are the tricks that will have guys begging not to leave your bed, they're also the secrets that all your friends wish you'd share. Whether you're practicing these with a regular date or wowing a first-time shag, the following acts are guaranteed to help you achieve sex perfection.

Come together: if this has happened as a mere fluke in the past, you'll have marveled at how good it felt to be that connected. Now you can achieve it as often as you want. To do this you need to understand how aroused you can both become and learn how to control each level of arousal, so that you both reach the same place at the same time. It may feel weird but you should try and express how turned on you are in stages, say numbers from one to ten. Remember, it's easier for men to become aroused more quickly—a man can orgasm within three minutes of becoming excited, but a woman needs a minimum of 13, so he might be at stage eight when you're only on stage three. Show each other how much stimulation you need to climax and figure out how long it takes each of you—this will take time and many sex sessions, but by coordinating your orgasms, you'll have double the pleasure.

Twice as much fun: what feels better than an orgasm? How about two, or maybe even three? Although multiple orgasms are the kind of thing you read about in sex manuals and hold the same mystical, not-quite-possible allure of a unicorn, they really can be yours. There are two ways to enjoy this sought-after experience, and here they are.

Make your orgasm a whole lot longer by strengthening your pelvic floor muscles. You can do this by learning to stop yourself mid-flow while going to the bathroom. Once you've got the hang of the "clench" practice it every day on your journey to work until those inner muscles are truly buff. Now, during sex, use those same muscles to grasp his penis inside you—this will send the blood flowing into your vagina. When you feel your first orgasm coming, resist the urge to let it happen. Instead, make him stay still, so that the tingly sensations just drift away. Continue to do this a few more times when your orgasm approaches—until you can't take it anymore. Finally, let the orgasm wash over you but, when it does, continue to clench and release your pelvic muscles the way you practiced—the extra flow of blood and pelvic contractions will increase and intensify your orgasm, giving you the longest, strongest sensations ever.

Another option is to continue pumping away together after your first orgasm. It may seem strange to continue going on after you've both reached your goal and it could even feel a bit sensitive at first, but after five or ten minutes, you will orgasm again. This time it might be a shorter, sweeter release, but hey, it's still two (or three if you continue) for the price of one.

TRY THIS NOW!

Write your own erotic fiction: type out a story starring your man and yourself. (Disguised, if you are scared someone will read it.) Leave it under his pillow one night. He'll love it. Just be careful not to get literal—describe his penis as "massive" and "engorged," not of "baby snail proportions."

Great handiwork

See a great hand job as the promise of things to come. This is your first chance to show off your sex skills, so get it just right. Start by positioning yourself in the best place, sit astride him or get him to stand in front of you. Stroke him lightly around his inner thighs and graze his penis with your fingertips until he becomes rock hard.

⟳ Then wrap your hand around the shaft of his penis and start rubbing up and down in a regular rhythm. As you get to the head close your fist a little when you glide over it, increasing the pressure—he has more nerve endings here so a stronger touch will drive him wild.

⟳ Use both hands on his penis at one time or use one hand to massage his balls. This way you can switch from hand to hand, when one gets numb. Keep a gliding motion rather than jerking, speed up for a while then slow down again, teasing him with that orgasm. The faster you move, the quicker he'll come, so speed up your pace for the grand finale. Once he has ejaculated, remove your hands straight away as he'll become ultra-sensitive and pleasure will quickly turn to pain with one tug too many.

⟳ The perfect blow job: tease him initially by nibbling along his thighs, then circling the head of his penis and running your tongue up and down the shaft. When you finally take his penis in your mouth place one hand at the base and use it to follow your lips, rubbing up and down the shaft with your hands and mouth simultaneously to increase the friction. Use the other hand to cup and massage his balls and lightly massage his perineum (the space between his testicles and his anus). Vary your speed and intensity, graze your teeth lightly over his skin, but never bite.

🌀 Suck on his balls and tweak his nipples. If you're worried about his penis going too far back into your throat and making you gag, guide it into the side of your mouth instead and if you need to come up for breath, tickle the frenulum (the small piece of skin where the head meets the shaft) with the end of your tongue at the same time (this area is extra sensitive).

🌀 The absolute best way you can drive a man wild is to act like you love what you're doing and there's nothing you enjoy more than having his cock in your mouth (a few pleasurable moans should do the trick). Oh, and if you can bring yourself to swallow, he'll think all his birthdays and Christmasses have come at once.

TRY THIS NOW!

An amazing alternative to the hand job is a boob job (and not the silicone variety). Place his penis between your breasts and squish them together so he can rub up and down between them. If your boobs are small and perky, crush them together as close as possible to create a cleavage for him to slide into. If you have voluptuous swingers, make this your specialty.

All the right moves

There's nothing wrong with a classic missionary screw once
in a while, but it's fun to shake it up a bit. You don't need to be an
Olympic athlete to master these gymnastic moves, but the more flexible
you are, the more creative your poses can be.

Woman on top

He can play with your breasts and clitoris, while you get to control the
speed and intensity of the experience, feeling him deep inside you. Make
things even more heated by squatting over him with your feet flat on the bed
and bouncing yourself up and down. Vary the position by facing the other
direction and letting him see the perfect curves of your butt—massage his
balls at the same time.

Doggy style

When a guy takes you from behind, his penis pushes against your
G-spot. Combine this with the fact that you can masturbate at the same
time and an orgasm is almost guaranteed. Switch things up by both
kneeling, or you kneel on the bed while he stands at the edge, or both
stand up and let him bend you over from the waist.

Standing up

If your man has been working out, let him show off his guns, by holding
you around his waist (do your bit by wrapping your legs over his hips
and clenching your thighs to keep yourself up there). This position means
deep penetration and amazing stimulation for your vaginal nerves. Not a
muscle man? Prop yourself up against a table or a wall instead.

Spooning

For those dozy mornings when cuddling leads to sex. This position allows you to play with your clitoris at the same time.

C.A.T.

The coital alignment technique increases your chance to orgasm together. He gets on top of you, lining his pelvis up against yours, so although the head of his penis is inside you, the shaft is pressing against your *mons pubis* (the fleshy mound covered in pubic hair). He steadies himself so his pelvis is never lower than yours and then you both rock in a synchronized motion. As you rock upward his penis slides down inside you, rubbing against your clitoris. During the downward stroke, he rocks slightly out of you again.

Sex sagas

It can't always be blissful between the sheets, and it helps to know how to deal with even the most awkward moments. Here are some solutions to those sticky situations.

S.T.I.s

Try and avoid S.T.I.s (sexually transmitted infections) in the first place by using condoms, as any rashes, skin disorders, or diseases can be painful, dangerous, and real mood killers. Avoid sex until all infections are cleared up. Don't assume just because you can't see symptoms you're good to go. Visit a gynecologist for regular check-ups.

Bondage

One girl's fantasy is another's nightmare. Being tied up and whipped could be a ton of fun, but stay in your comfort zone by choosing silk scarves over handcuffs (they're more comfortable and easier to remove), having a "safe" word that you'll use when you want the session to end, and only indulging with someone you really trust.

Boredom

Same position, same location, same time of day? Shake things up a bit and add some spontaneity to your sex. After reading this chapter you'll have a few new tips and tricks to try out.

Premature ejaculation

To increase the length of time your man can have sex, grasp the base of his penis and squeeze firmly when he's about to come. This will stop the flow of semen from his testicles and delay his orgasm.

Threesomes

Only invite a friend along if it's something you're both into (don't just do it for him). For many, three's a crowd, so establish some ground rules first, also consider how it may affect your friendships afterward.

Saying the wrong name

Oops! If you think he might not have heard, focus his attention immediately elsewhere with any mind-blowing sex act before he has time to mull it over. But if you're well and truly busted, laugh it off with as much style and panache as you can muster.

Feeling freaked out

Sex is only fun when you're both enjoying yourselves. Although you should never feel bad about what turns you on, it's different strokes for different folks. The only way to let someone know what you're cool with doing in bed and to find out what they're comfortable with, is to communicate. Never do anything that makes you feel uncomfortable, but equally don't insist anyone else does either.

Going tantric

You've probably heard many an Eastern promise about this method of sex, but have you ever tried it for yourself? To make a mystic commitment and share the tantric sex experience together, start by lying naked, facing each other and discovering your body parts without arousing each other.

Once you have done that, lie spooning each other and listening to your breath. Synchronize your breathing so that you inhale for four seconds, hold for four seconds, exhale for four seconds, and pause for four seconds. Repeat this until you are in total harmony and try to imagine your breath is entering you through your vagina and being expelled through your mouth, while he visualizes that same breath entering his mouth and leaving through his penis. This connects your chakras (the spot in between your eyebrows) and creates a circle of energy between you. After a while, turn to face each other and stare into each other's third eyes (chakras) for a few minutes.

Now sit on top of him, facing each other with your legs wrapped around his back and let him enter you. Now you do nothing, except gaze into each other's third eyes and synchronize your breathing, as before. While in this position, flex your pelvic floor muscles (which sends blood into your vagina), he does the same, rushing blood into his penis. Marvelously, even without thrusting you'll find yourself becoming aroused and reaching a level of intense pleasure. Continue to breathe and relax and wait for the next, higher, level of sensation. This will go on for a while . . . until you both finally experience the most intense, mind-blowing orgasms ever—it's definitely worth the wait.

Sensual games

If you thought we'd already covered all the kinky ways to spice up your sex life, you were wrong. These games will get you hornier than you ever thought possible . . .

Force fields

Start naked, facing each other. Pretend there is a force field all around your bodies, which is two inches from your skin—so you can stroke each other, or pretend to massage each other's sexual organs, but you can't actually touch. The feeling of having someone almost connect with your body intensifies your cravings for their touch. Sooner or later someone will break the rules—which will make them the loser— although at this stage you will be so overcome with hard-core lust, you will both be winners.

Two blind mice

When neither of you can see each other's bodies you have to rely so much more on your other senses: touch, smell, sound, and taste. This sexual encounter will have you licking your way to each other's hot spots and relying on moans and groans to know you're getting it right.

Sets of nine

Give your sex organs a massage with this Taoist technique. Let him put just the head of his penis inside you and do nine short, shallow thrusts, then one deep one where he puts the entire length inside you. Then repeat again, this time with eight shallow strokes and two deep ones at the end. Repeat once more, this time with seven shallow strokes and three deep. Continue until you end with one shallow stroke and nine deep. Bliss.

Nervous

Just like the game you used to play at school, but this one's more hardcore. One person starts making some slow sexual moves, while the other assesses whether the situation is making them "nervous." This is a perfect way to explore your kinkier desires, from anal stimulation to dildos to bondage. See how he feels about your lubricated finger being pushed slowly into his butt hole. See how much you like having a strap-on eased inside you.

Blue movie

Rig up the camera to a TV and play it through the screen. Do not, repeat, not, insert a tape. All those urban myths about mixing the tape up with another and playing it when your parents come to stay? They're true. Instead, think of a theme, dress up, and turn your room into the scene from a sexy—or just plain blue —movie.

TRY THIS NOW!

Taste Sensation: add a little flavor to your sex life by raiding the refrigerator. Drizzle honey over your nipples and let him lick it off. Squirt whipped cream into his butt crack and glide your tongue along until you've slurped it all up. Crack open a bottle of Champagne and trickle it over your clitoris.

WHEN THE GOING GETS TOUGH

How to survive any situation

8

When life ain't so smooth

Finding success on the dating scene is about finding happiness in the rest of your life, but things don't always go the way you'd like them to. Sometimes life can be pretty crappy—just when everything else in your world falls into place, there's one thing that screws it up. It could be a harrowing break-up with the guy you thought was your soul mate, getting laid off from a great job, having an infuriating bust-up with your parents, or realizing you are so far into the red that you can't remember a time when you were debt-free. Sadly, no one is immune to life's foul-ups, but the important thing is knowing how to handle them.

There are those tiny things that can really bug you—a snippy argument with a close friend, a tear in your favorite pants, gaining a few pounds. Taken one at a time, these are the kinds of things you can shrug off, but a day of them (especially a pre-menstrual day) can seem like the end of the world. Face these problems head on—after you've had a chance quietly to seethe and curse suck it up and rectify these minor impositions as quickly as you can.

Then there's the big sh*t. Losing your job, accruing horrifying debt, accidentally becoming pregnant, a nasty end to a good friendship, divorce, death. This is the stuff that is going to take a lot more time—emotionally and literally—to come to terms with.

In any kind of hardship, it's important that you acknowledge your lows and recognize that the only way is up and that you intend to get there with as much dignity and grace as possible. There's no such thing as "wallowing" in your misery—you should do your crying in private, or at least in the arms of your closest friend or partner.

Stay positive

Don't crawl into a hole and hope it will all go away—rise to the occasion. You must be determined to overcome it, trying to find a way to make things better. If you don't find it as easy to get peppy again, surround yourself with practical, positive friends who will happily help you find that silver lining and focus on the problem solving.

Don't be passive

You know where you want to go and what you want to achieve. But when things are harder than you expected, don't give up. At times like this you need to make use of every opportunity to improve and learn from the situation and make the most of every contact that comes your way.

Put yourself out there and seize every opportunity— missing out is not an option. At every party, bar, dinner make sure you think about the contacts you could make. Don't wait for people to discover you, because it won't ever happen. You have to get out there and show them what you've got.

"Just don't give up trying to do what you really want to do. Where there is love and inspiration, I don't think you can go wrong."

ELLA FITZGERALD

Rising to the challenge

Being brave and dealing with tough situations is a surefire way to boost your confidence. Different things freak out different people— a party where you don't know anyone, a blind date, skydiving— whatever makes your knees knock is worth trying once. Again, don't expect this to be a walk in the park: You will feel scared, but that's the point.

The exhilaration you'll experience once you've completed your task will make it all worthwhile. Don't stop there, though. Keep pushing yourself, watch your confidence grow, and take pleasure in kicking your fear in the butt.

Every time you do something that makes you feel good—write it down. If you can't think of anything more tedious than writing a journal, keep a mini-notebook in your bag instead and just jot down a few words each time. It can be anything: you called your grandmother, you avoided the 3P.M. doughnut craving, you bought a cup of coffee for a homeless person. When you're feeling blue, flick through your list and remind yourself of the things you feel good about.

This works the other way around too. At your lowest moments, make a note of what's getting you down. When you're feeling more rational, read through your entries and look for a pattern. If you discover you're generally unhappy with one area of your life or at certain times in your life (P.M.S. anyone?) you can work with the information and try to do something about it.

Love and war

Even the best of relationships hits stony ground once in a while.
There are naturally going to be times when you don't see eye to eye,
or your beau does something to really enrage you. Depending on
how long you've been together and how much you like the guy, you
have two choices, either to dump him, or to work through it together.

If you choose the latter, you'll need to bear some things in mind.
The first is communication, which is essential. Refusing to call him
until he apologizes may work, but could also leave you single again.
Calmly discussing how you both feel is more likely to help you reach
a solution. Remember, men are generally useless at discussing their
feelings so this may not be a cinch, but you should get there in the
end. Compromise is important, but so is staying true to your beliefs;
evaluate every issue that comes between you and try to find a
resolution that suits you both. Some things will never change and
these will be the things you either learn to live with or that eventually
get the better of you.

Once you have your man hooked, you want him to stay that way.
Keeping the relationship hot means not getting stuck in a rut or
letting things slide. Remember what attracted you to each other in
the first place—your adventurous spirit, your sex appeal, your
attitude and ideas. Maintain these elements of your character and five
years together will still seem like five days. Be spontaneous!

🌀 Book random weekends away.

🌀 Do crazy things together (Have you ever ridden a trapeze?).

🌀 Spend a day naked.

🌀 Order sushi and let him eat it off your belly.

🌀 Relive the flirting techniques that caught him in the first place.

🌀 Make a Saturday night date together and each arrange part of the night—one choosing a restaurant, the other making after-dinner plans.

Budget

Send him a lacy thong in a box wrapped in brown paper. Attach a parcel tag stating the time and location that you intend to wear it.

He'll set his alarm the moment he receives it.

Blowout

Book a weekend in Hawaii. Slip into a grass skirt, order your favorite cocktail, and watch the sun set before embarking on a night of unbridled Polynesian passion.

Ciao baby

"I say goodbye to love." "Every time we say goodbye, I cry a little." "Bye, bye love." It's a lot easier to sing about splitting up with a guy than actually to do it. But sometimes you have to bite the bullet. You know you're too good to date a scumbag, and even if he hasn't actually wronged you, there are still times when "so long" are the only words you should utter. Here are a few of them.

🌀 When he's two-timing you: never share your men. If he's into playing the field it's time to relegate him to the bench.

🌀 When he disses you: you're pretty amazing and if he doesn't get that, he's the one with the problem. Anyone who regularly criticizes your body, clothes, personality, or lifestyle isn't worth having around.

🌀 When he doesn't live up to his promises: if he talks the talk, he'd better walk the walk. Everyone loves weekends away, gifts, and regular phone calls, but if all you're actually receiving is the promise of these things, don't hold your breath any longer.

🌀 When he's going nowhere: struggling artists—gorgeous, wannabe rock stars—adorable. But at what point are you going to stop paying the check and acting like his personal assistant? Vibrant, determined women deserve men with the same attitude, so don't waste your time with a dead-end guy.

The art of dumping with dignity

Basically, there is no easy way to dump anyone, be they male or female. You are saying "I no longer like/fancy you enough to continue wanting an intimate relationship with you" which is bad news however it is put. If you're the one doing the dumping, it's only too easy to fall into the trap of making gentle hints and being increasingly unavailable in the hope that you'll let him down gently. But it's painful and confusing to be on the end of such arbitrary behavior. Instead follow these hints to make a clean and fair break.

Don't give him the silent treatment

Well, you wouldn't like it if he did that to you would you—it's just
plain bad manners? If you've been on a few dates with him and got
up to all sorts of shenanigans in the bedroom, you should be able to
tell him you don't want to see him again, no matter how nerve
racking it is. Treat him with respect and be prepared to answer
his questions.

Do give him a reason

You don't have to give him the real reason for losing you—his
irritating friends, the second rate sex, his terrible breath and the oh-
so-loud snoring—but you do need to offer a reason that is plausible
and that he can take away, his dignity intact. Be diplomatic though—
don't make him feel as though there is something physically or
emotionally wrong with him, and don't make him feel he did
something that turned you off.

Often, your reason may be more to do with not feeling a spark
than something that is clearer cut. But this is still a plausible reason,
even if it's difficult to pin down precisely. Try saying "I don't know
why, but despite having a great time, I don't feel strongly enough for
you and I don't think that's fair because you deserve better."

Do shed a few tears

This part is about leaving his ego intact. We're not talking weeping buckets, we're just saying a few well-timed tears will leave him thinking the relationship meant something to you too, even if it didn't. Flinging your arms open with relief can wait until he's gone.

Don't do it over dinner

Choose your venue carefully. Over dinner in a candle-lit restaurant is not the place to tell someone you don't want to see them again. Public places in general are difficult because he might get emotional. Instead, ask him to meet you in a local park or go for a walk along the river or seafront. Walking side by side reduces the intensity of a face to face showdown, and at the end of the walk you can hop on the bus back home. Alone.

Do look your worst

Whatever it was that drew him to you in the first place, make sure it's long gone. If you showed up for your first date in spiky heels and a low cut revealing top, turn up in a dowdy pullover without any makeup on. OK, so this lasting image of you might not be in keeping with your femme fatale image, but this bit is about making life easier for him!

Don't fall into bed with him

No matter what the temptation, there's no point succumbing to one last romp just for old times' sake. Don't forget men use sex as a measure of love and affection and you'll only leave him confused, and put yourself right back at square one. Don't give him false hope that you'll change your mind.

Dealing with being dumped

We all get knock-backs—where a man's not interested or doesn't ring again after the first date or two. These are often hurtful, confidence-shattering moments. Take time to get the guy out of your system, whether it's with a couple of black and white movies or a cocktail or two in a swanky bar. But part of dating confidently is to know that these knock-backs aren't the end of the world, even if you were secretly planning the wedding in your head.

The best thing to do is to pick yourself up, dust yourself down and get back out there as soon as you can. Perhaps forget about men for a couple of weeks and focus on friends you've been neglecting during your whirlwind romance.

Remember, if things didn't work out it was for a good reason and it will be better for you both in the long run. Stay optimistic—remember that there are plenty more date opportunities just around the next corner, and that his lack of interest doesn't reflect personally on you.

"I was dumped three months ago and am still finding it very difficult. We only dated for six weeks, but I miss him so much. For my own good, I desperately need to move on, but he's all I can think about."

KERRY, 23

Unlucky in love

If relationships were easy, country singers would have nothing to write about and great aunts wouldn't be able patronizingly to mutter, "more fish in the sea" or "it's better to have loved and lost . . . " Here are a few of the crappy things you could have to face on the way to finding your perfect (or almost perfect) guy.

Sayonara sweetie: being dumped sucks, but it's okay, it's good to wallow in your depression for a few days. Loll around in your flannel PJs, play the weepiest love ballads, eat Frosties straight from the box— mourn the end of the relationship. When you've had enough of feeling sad, rally your friends around you and go out more, take up new pursuits, be open to meeting people. Accept that even if it's tough at first you will move on and the most valuable things you've taken from the relationship are experience and enlightenment. You're one step closer to finding someone worthy of you.

The wrong guy: why do some of us just seem to attract the bad guys? He seemed so great in the beginning . . . or maybe he didn't and that's subconsciously what attracted you to him. Decide if the reason you pick these kind of men to date is because you know ultimately they are wrong for you and you won't have to think about anything long-term. If you're positive you're not a commitment-phobe, the next step is to date guys who aren't your type. Of course, you've got to find him the teeniest bit attractive, but if creative types attract you, then end up being too self absorbed, try dating a banker. Or if you're lured by the spunky nature of a jock, but eventually find him too laddish, an artsy guy could have the sensitivity you've been missing.

Wanting what you can't have: nothing is more infuriating than meeting the man of your dreams . . . and finding out he's already taken. Or that he doesn't feel the same way about you. The truth is, this is a no-win situation, whichever way you look at it. Never steal another woman's man (too tacky for words) and do you really want to be with a guy who doesn't totally adore you back? Sure, he could grow to love you, but let him do that in his own time, while you continue to play the field.

Cheating heart: having your heart broken is hard enough, but when it's because he's slept with someone else the pain is almost intolerable. Most people really can't get past this. Once your trust has been abused it can be beyond difficult to return to normality again. So you have two choices: dump him or try to move past it together. You probably can't forgive him, and he shouldn't expect you to. Try and communicate how you feel and don't let him put any blame on you—this was all him.

Pick-me-ups

Whatever it is that has ruined your day, you cannot let it get you down forever. Here are ten ways to raise your spirits (splash out on the blowout suggestions, or bash your blues bargain-basement-style with the budget suggestions).

Budget

- Dance in the rain. Leave your umbrella at home, twirl through the puddles and let yourself get totally soaked—then warm up again in a long, soothing bath.

- Bake a cake from scratch—there's something cathartic about baking (and not from a mix), plus your kitchen will smell divine. Once you're done, treat yourself to a huge guilt-free slice.

- Go to bed early. Take a big glass of wine, or a mug of hot chocolate and a few un-opened magazines. Spend the next few hours flicking and sipping.

- Buy your favorite movie on video (the funnier the better) when you're feeling blue, put it on and get lost in that world for a while.

- Find some water—the sea, a lake, a swimming pool, even a puddle. Sit and reflect or dive right in (not the puddle). Water draws out the negative ions from your body, so you're left with only positives.

Blowout

- Rent a convertible for a day. Put the top down, pump up the music and feel the wind whistle through your hair.

- Plan a weekend away with your best friends. Take the train, find a family-run B&B, and stay up all night talking.

- Take a lunch hour, when you'd normally stay at your desk. Go to a fancy restaurant and order a lovely meal for one, take a newspaper. Or sit in the park for an hour with a good book. Or splurge on a pair of party shoes that you just can't resist.

- Buy little gifts for each of your friends. Focusing the attention on them will take your mind off your woes and making others happy in turn brightens your day.

- Get a lavish beauty treatment like an aromatherapy wrap or a massage. Even if you can't see the effects of these treatments, you'll certainly feel them. Bliss!

CONQUER
THE WORLD

Use your charms to help you achieve anything

9

How to have it all

What's the secret to having anything you want? The truth is, there isn't just one answer to this: to pursue your dreams you need different types of ammo under your belt. A crucial one is flirting. As you know, a femme fatale doesn't just flirt with men, women can also fall prey to her flattery and alluring tactics.

You should use your charm and charisma to help you achieve anything you want—whether that's a job promotion, a legendary soirée, or a discount on a vacation.

Sweet-talking isn't the only thing you'll need to use—there's that confidence thing again—but hard work and talent are also essential. To get anywhere (or anything) in life, you have to start with determination and drive. If you want it enough, it will come. Then you need the will power to remain constant in your battle to get what you deserve (and you do deserve it). With a few clever tricks up your sleeve everything will be a cinch—it's guaranteed.

Working girl

Let's start by saying, no matter how sexy you are, and how irresistible men are to your charms, a femme fatale will never sleep her way to the top. It's just not classy—it's so much more chic to get there on your own merits. Having said that, you can use a few of your natural talents to help you climb a rung or two of the job ladder.

When it comes down to it, practically every employer on this planet is looking for someone smart, reliable, and trustworthy. What makes you stand out from the rest of the crowd is your sparkle and enthusiasm. Start as you mean to go on and show any boss-to-be that you're already ahead of the game. Say you have to fulfill some kind of brief as part of an interview. Instead of simply doing what is required to complete the task, why not think up ways of taking it further and putting a few additional ideas into your submission? It will be far more than is needed, but it will get you the job. The reason why? It's always better to do too much than too little. Prospective employers are looking for that person willing to go the extra mile, so make sure it's you.

When asking for a raise, learn to be an ace-negotiator. Explain the reasons why you deserve a raise (these should include extra responsibilities you've taken on that weren't in your job description) and find out how much money is usually paid to a person in your position.

The tough news is, most people are ready for a promotion long before the bigwigs see fit to give it to them. Before you ask for one, make sure you've done everything you can do to earn a new title. This should include: asking for more responsibilities, staying late to get extra work done (and to show you're committed) and finding out what the new position entails so you're prepared for what you'll be taking on.

*"There is no point at which you can say,
Well I'm successful now. I might as well take a nap."*
CARRIE FISHER

On the subject of relationships at work, having frissons with every man in your office is definitely not advised. Try to curb some of your flirtier techniques (no pressing him up against the water cooler) and simply see men as colleagues. If this is absolutely impossible and you just have to get intimate with one of your coworkers, keep your personal and professional lives separate. Save the pet names, making out, and arguments for home.

There will always come a time when you have to move on. No job is going to be stimulating all of the time, but if you've got to the stage where you can do yours with your eyes closed, ask for more work or different challenges. As soon as you feel you've mastered what you're doing, hunt for something new—even if this means a brand new job. Treading water is eventually going to leave you uninspired and unfulfilled.

Get the job you really want

- Use your contacts—friends, friends of friends, family friends, and previous employers.

- Network at graduate fairs, work socials, and sales conferences.

- Be proactive and set up your own networking community through websites.

- Talk to a careers advisor.

- Find out if you can get an intercompany transfer.

The green-eyed monster

Jealousy is one of the worst feelings ever. Whether you resent another woman, or she's envious of you, it's a no-win situation. So let's start with quashing your own green-eyed monster. Jealousy stems from insecurity and low self-esteem. Hopefully, most of the time, you're confident and content, but on those occasions you feel the envy rising, check yourself.

What is making you feel this way? Is it something you too can achieve or are you craving something totally out of your reach? It is true that a little competitive rivalry compels you to do better, work harder, reach further, but only if you can keep a sense of proportion about it. Jealousy is ugly, but drive and desire are things worth finding within the emotion. If your feelings are making you miserable, the best thing to do is face them head on. Tell the person of whom you are envious how you feel and why—chances are there are aspects of your life/character/body that she's equally impressed by—things you might have forgotten you even had going for you. Getting your feelings out in the open will hopefully diminish them or at least boost your own self-esteem. If you can't face your foe, reveal that jade-eyed monster to your close friends instead, for the morale boost you need.

When someone is being bitchy and catty toward you—and you have a pretty good idea it stems from jealousy—take the higher ground. It is far more graceful to ignore the snide comments and instead win her over with your warmth and charm. Don't bite back, but go to the other extreme and tell her what you admire about her. Your flattery should make her feel more self-assured and crush her caustic feelings.

Up, up, and away . . .

It should not be underestimated just how important it is for you to spread your wings. As a glorious, open-minded woman you need to fill your head with new places, exciting experiences, and to become inspired by femmes fatales the world over. The more money you can put aside, the better.

Remember to do your homework before you set your manicured foot onto foreign soils, however. This means buying a good travel guide and retiring for a long soak in the bath. Also, attempt to learn the lingo. A phrase book should suffice for the essentials ("How much is it?" and "Where is the bathroom?" at least) before you go.

Once you have secured an upgrade on your flight, there are a few other tricks for making the journey a whole lot more comfortable, (a pair of velour sweatpants packed in your hand luggage, for example). Alcohol may be free but will leave you dehydrated and groggy, so stick to water and bring a bag of trail mix to nibble on instead of the bland airplane fare. As soon as you have charmed the check-in staff, wipe off your make-up and replace with a layer of thick moisturizer (to combat the hard-core air conditioning) and avoid D.V.T. (deep vein thrombosis) by doing a few yoga stretches in the aisle whenever you get the chance.

When in Rome . . . or Barcelona, or Paris, or Marrakech, take lifestyle props from the locals. The only way to immerse yourself in their culture is to leave your normal routine at home. So sample the different dishes, steer clear of tourist traps, and befriend a few locals to take you sightseeing.

Be savvy

You don't need to be rolling in cash to live like you're mega-rich. Wow others with your thrifty methods of getting what they want. Here are some tips to help you on your way to the good life. Get more bang for your buck.

On vacation

When booking your jaunt to sunnier climes, first find your dream location, then hunt for the cheapest deal. The prices quoted in holiday brochures are always inflated so refuse to pay that amount. Speak to travel agents and ask what deal they can get for you, or search online for special offers. For last minute trips you can barter even more and check out the websites dedicated to securing you a flight and hotel for a shockingly rock-bottom price.

On airplanes

Dressing nicely used to be the best way to get an upgrade, now being a member of the airline's frequent-flyer program is a surer bet that you'll be looked at favorably (signing up is free). Smart threads still cut it—as does a polite request (act entitled and you won't stand a chance). If an upgrade is out of the question, early birds can ask to sit by an exit, which means a ton more legroom (it also helps if you have a 6' 4" boyfriend!).

In restaurants

Book well in advance to ensure you'll snag a reservation. Scope out the joint beforehand so you can request a particular table. If the prices are just too high for your budget, ask if they have a prix fixe menu, or order two appetizers (usually half the price of an entrée) and insist you have a small appetite. Prices are often reduced at lunchtime too.

In shops

Check if your favorite store has a mailing list—most do and once you're on it, you'll be kept up to date with sales and offered discounts. Make friends with a sales assistant, always get her to serve you, and build a rapport. She'll probably waiver a no-hold policy for you and may even call when new items come in. (Buddy up with the store's manager and it's your lucky day.)

In beauty stores

Swanky beauty counters don't appreciate scroungers, so don't march up to the counter and expect them to dole out free samples. On the other hand, you could splash out on a soap (usually one of the cheapest products available), enquire about other items, and end up going home with a bag of samples.

Be smart, be sassy, be safe

Here's how . . .

- ✹ Always save enough cash for the entire cab fare home—including the tip.

- ✹ Whenever going somewhere new, buy a map and get as familiar with your surroundings as possible.

- ✹ Don't jog with a personal CD player on, as it stops you being alert and aware of what's going on around you.

- ✹ Keep your cell phone fully charged—you never know when you may need it.

- ✹ Never collect your car from a multi-storey car park at night alone—cough up the extra for a valet.

- ✹ Learn where your fuse box is in your apartment before a blackout.

- ✹ Let at least one person know where you are at all times.

- ✹ Travel light—if you can fit your wheeled luggage case into an overhead compartment you'll never have to stand in line at lost and found again.

🌀 Keep precious jewelry somewhere random, like in an egg carton in the fridge or stuffed in an old sock—where no burglar would ever think to look.

🌀 Never go to sleep with your lavender-scented aromatherapy candle still burning.

🌀 Learn how to change a tire—you never know when it might come in useful.

🌀 Don't go home with a total stranger—no matter how hot he is.

🌀 Take self-defense classes. If you never end up using them, even better.

🌀 When traveling abroad always carry around the details of the place where you're staying and learn how to ask, "donde esta?" in the appropriate language.

🌀 Carry an alarm—the noise will hopefully scare away any potential attacker and alert everyone else's attention.

Congratulations!!

You are a femme fatale and a dating guru! You are one of those women men gaze at and women admire. You're a female who knows what she wants and understands what makes her happy.

You actively work to keep your body strong, fit, and healthy and you accept (and even sometimes adore) your reflection. Your style is phenomenal, because you have the daring and dash to wear exactly what suits you.

Guys are entranced by your charms and even if you haven't yet found the one who knocks your socks off, you certainly have a line of them willing to try. And for the lucky few who make it to the sack with you, your new, improved sex skills will mean earth-shattering orgasms for the both of you.

Your career path is lined with roses now that you know how to get that promotion and negotiate the salary that is yours for the taking. You also have the sass and street smarts to make the other areas of your existence run smoothly—including your relationships, home, and social life. And hey, if the sh*t hits the fan every once in a while—you even know how to handle that with skill and grace. You're a hell of a lady—you should be proud.

Now let's keep it that way . . .